Hello, Family Members,

Learning to read is one of the most important accomplishments of early childhood. **Hello Reader!** books are designed to help children become skilled readers who like to read. Beginning readers learn to read by remembering frequently used words like "the," "is," and "and"; by using phonics skills to decode new words; and by interpreting picture and text clues. These books provide both the stories children enjoy and the structure they need to read fluently and independently. Here are suggestions for helping your child *before, during,* and *after* reading:

Before

- Look at the cover and pictures and have your child predict what the story is about.
- Read the story to your child.
- Encourage your child to chime in with familiar words and phrases.
- Echo read with your child by reading a line first and having your child read it after you do.

During

- Have your child think about a word he or she does not recognize right away. Provide hints such as "Let's see if we know the sounds" and "Have we read other words like this one?"
- Encourage your child to use phonics skills to sound out new words.
- Provide the word for your child when more assistance is needed so that he or she does not struggle and the experience of reading with you is a positive one.
- Encourage your child to have fun by reading with a lot of expression . . . like an actor!

After

- Have your child keep lists of interesting and favorite words.
- Encourage your child to read the books over and over again. Have him or her read to brothers, sisters, grandparents, and even teddy bears. Repeated readings develop confidence in young readers.
- Talk about the stories. Ask and answer questions. Share ideas about the funniest and most interesting characters and events in the stories.

I do hope that you and your child enjoy this book.

— Francie Alexander
Chief Educati(
Scholastic's L(

To Katie and Rachel,
bright stars in my galaxy

— R.H.

To my mother, Elizabeth,
my father, Thomas, and to my three wonderful
sisters, Lee, Bernardine, and Mary

— G.H.

Go to scholastic.com for web site information on
Scholastic authors and illustrators.

ISBN 0-439-32100-X

Library of Congress Cataloging-in-Publication Data

Hansen, Rosanna
        Seeing Stars / by Rosanna Hansen; illustrated by Greg Harris.
        p. cm.
        Summary: Describes the place of our solar system in the Milky Way galaxy and some of the constellations that can be seen from Earth.
        ISBN 0-439-32100-X
        1. Constellations—Juvenile literature. 2. Milky Way—Juvenile literature. [1. Constellations. 2. Astronomy.]
        I. Harris, Greg, 1950- ill. II. Title.

        QB802.H355 2002
        523.8—dc21   2001049673

10 9 8 7 6 5 4 3   03 04 05 06
                        Printed in the U.S.A.   23
                        First printing, May 2002

Seeing Stars

The Milky Way and Its Constellations

by Rosanna Hansen
Illustrated by Greg Harris

Hello Reader! Science — Level 4

SCHOLASTIC INC.

New York   Toronto   London   Auckland   Sydney
Mexico City   New Delhi   Hong Kong   Buenos Aires

CHAPTER ONE

SEEING STARS

If you look at the sky on a clear night, how many stars can you see? Hundreds? Thousands?

Scientists say you can see as many as 3,000 stars with your eyes alone. With a telescope, you can see 600,000 stars or more!

Stars look like tiny, twinkling lights to us. They look small because they are very, very far away. They twinkle because we see them through the air and dust surrounding Earth.

Stars are huge balls of hot, fiery gases. Inside a star, hot gases squeeze tightly together. This squeezing makes the center of a star incredibly hot. It is like a giant atomic furnace. And the hotter a star is, the more brightly it glows.

Our sun is a star. It is not the biggest or brightest star in the universe, but it is the closest star to our planet Earth. Still, the sun is about 93 million miles away from us!

Imagine you were in a spaceship traveling 30,000 miles an hour. It would take you over four months to reach the sun.

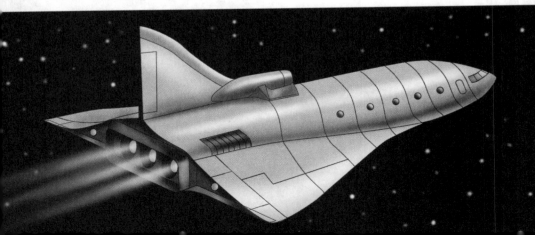

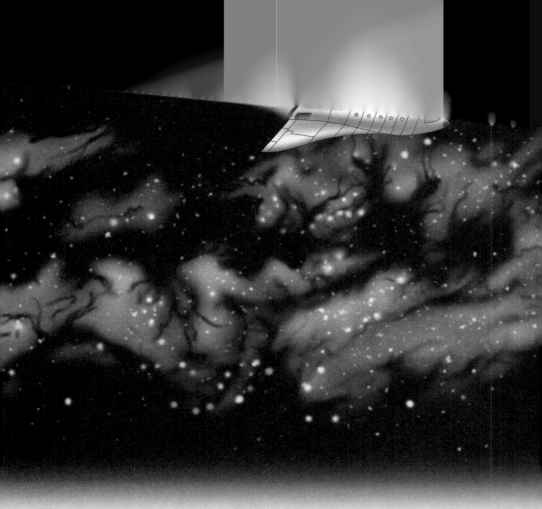

After the sun, our nearest star is *Alpha Centauri.* It is about 25 trillion miles away! Your spaceship would take about 95,000 years to reach this star. The light from Alpha Centauri takes about 4$\frac{1}{2}$ years to reach Earth. When you look at Alpha Centauri, you are seeing light that left the star about 4$\frac{1}{2}$ years ago.

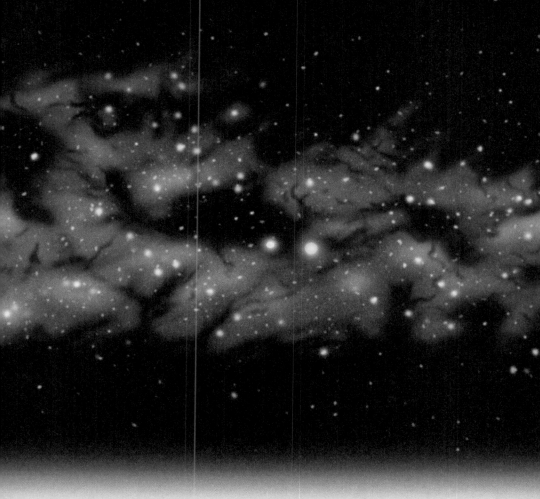

After Alpha Centauri, the other stars are much, much farther away. Some of them are millions of trillions of miles from Earth. With these amazing distances, no one knows exactly how many stars there are in all. But most astronomers think that there are about 200 billion stars in the universe!

CHAPTER TWO

THE MILKY WAY GALAXY

On a clear summer night, you can see a pale band of light spreading across the sky. Long ago, no one knew what this band of light could be. The ancient Greeks said that it was made of milk. They said that baby Hercules had spilled his milk across the sky! That is why we call this band of light the *Milky Way*.

With a telescope, we can see that the Milky Way is really a huge cloud of stars, or a *galaxy*. A galaxy is a giant collection of stars, dust, and gas. The stars in the Milky Way are so far away that they blend into one glowing band of light.

The Milky Way contains more than one hundred billion stars! Because our sun is one of the stars in the Milky Way galaxy, that makes the Milky Way our home in space.

Do you know your space address? It looks like this:

Your Name
Earth
Solar System
Milky Way Galaxy
Universe

The Milky Way galaxy is shaped like a huge pinwheel, or spiral. Its glowing center has curving arms that sweep out into space.

Our sun and *solar system* are out near the edge of one of these arms. The solar system is made up of our sun and all of the objects that travel around it. These objects include the nine planets and their moons, comets, asteroids, and meteorites. Our planet, Earth, is one of the nine planets that travels around the sun.

From the side, our galaxy looks like a huge flying saucer. It has a big bump in the center of a thin, flat disk.

Our sun and solar system travel slowly around the center of the Milky Way galaxy. It takes our sun 250 million years to go all the way around!

The Milky Way galaxy is only one of millions of galaxies in the universe. No one knows for sure how many galaxies there are in all. Most astronomers think there are at least a hundred billion galaxies.

Like the Milky Way, some galaxies have a spiral shape. Other galaxies have egg-like, or *elliptical,* shapes. And some galaxies don't have much shape at all, so they are called *irregular* galaxies.

CHAPTER THREE

WHAT ARE CONSTELLATIONS?

Thousands of years ago, people often watched the stars at night. They thought that groups of stars formed pictures in the sky. In some groups, people saw the shapes of animals. In others, they saw the shapes of their gods or heroes.

Sometimes people made up stories about these star pictures. The stories helped them remember each star picture and its place in the sky. We call these star pictures *constellations*.

Many of the constellations we know today were named by the ancient Greeks and Romans. Astronomers have added some new constellations, too. There are 88 constellations in all.

No one can see all 88 constellations at one time. You can only see the constellations shining above your part of the world.

Before compasses were invented, people used constellations to help find their way. Sailors learned to steer their ships using constellations as a guide. Explorers watched for the *North Star* or the constellation known as the *Big Dipper* to keep from getting lost.

Constellations helped ancient people keep
track of the seasons, too. Long ago, people
noticed that some constellations seem to
move when the seasons changed. So they
learned to use the constellations as a
calendar. Farmers learned to plant their
crops when the spring constellations
appeared. They harvested when the fall
constellations came into view.

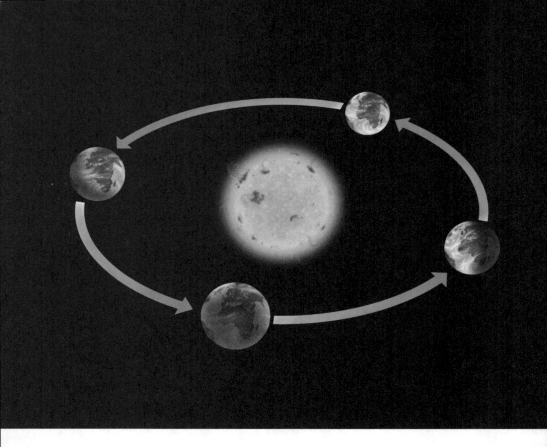

Today, we know that constellations aren't really moving in the sky. Instead, Earth is moving. It takes one year for Earth to travel around the sun. As Earth travels, the constellations seem to change position. Some constellations, such as the one called *Leo*, can only be seen during part of the year. Others, including the *Great Bear*, can be seen all year long. The year-round constellations change position in the sky as the seasons change.

Here is the way the Great Bear looks during different seasons:

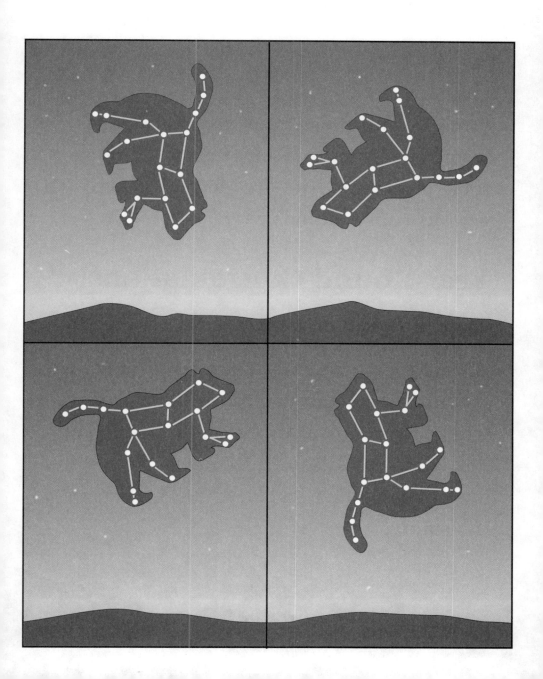

CHAPTER FOUR

THE CONSTELLATIONS

Stories of how many constellations were formed come from Greek myths. Here are some of these stories and descriptions of various constellations.

Year-Round Constellations

Ursa Major: The Great Bear

Zeus, king of the gods, once fell in love with a beautiful woman named Callisto. Zeus's wife was jealous of Callisto and tried to hurt her. To keep Callisto safe, Zeus changed her into a bear. Then he placed her high among the stars.

Within the Great Bear, you can see seven stars that seem to form a ladle, or dipper. This group of stars is the *Big Dipper*. The two stars at the end of the Big Dipper's bowl are called the *pointer stars*. They always point to a very important star called the North Star, or *Polaris*.

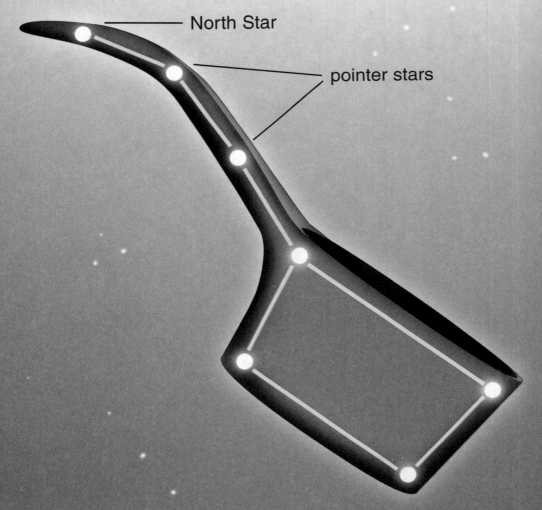

North Star

pointer stars

For thousands of years, people all over the world have watched the Big Dipper. Sometimes they've had different ideas about this group of stars. The ancient Vikings thought the Big Dipper looked like a wagon. In China, people said it was a royal chariot. And in England today, people say the Big Dipper looks like a plow.

In the southern United States, the Big Dipper used to be called the *Drinking Gourd*. Over a hundred years ago, people in the south sometimes had gourds for water dippers. At that time, there was still slavery in the south. Slaves who wanted to escape often followed the Drinking Gourd at night to help them find their way north to freedom.

Ursa Minor: Little Bear

The *Little Bear* is the son of Callisto, the Great Bear. After Zeus changed Callisto into a large bear, he changed Callisto's son into a young bear. Then he took the two bears by their stumpy tails. He swung them one by one up into the heavens! And that is how their tails were stretched so long. To this day, the bears roam the heavens together.

The stars in the Little Bear constellation are small and dim. This makes the Little Bear harder to find than many constellations.

Within the Little Bear, you can see the stars that form the *Little Dipper*. The three stars of the bear's tail form the Little Dipper's handle.

The brightest star in the Little Bear is the North Star. The North Star is the only star that never seems to move at all. It always remains almost exactly north. All the other stars seem to circle around the North Star. For thousands of years, people have used the North Star to help them find their way.

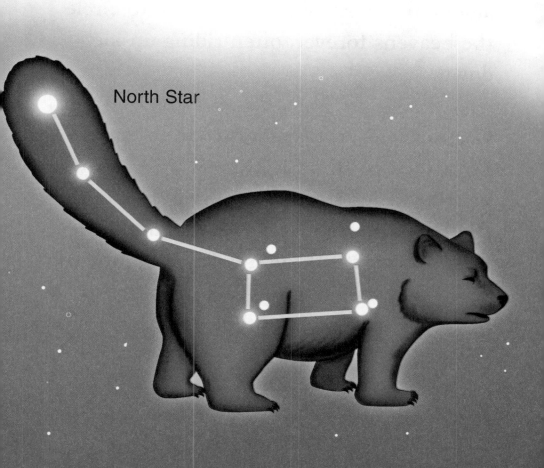

North Star

Cassiopeia

Cassiopeia was a famous queen. She was known far and wide for her great beauty. One day, the queen boasted that she was more beautiful than the sea nymphs. The sea god heard Cassiopeia boasting. He grew angry and decided to teach her a lesson. To punish her, the sea god placed Cassiopeia among the stars. She was doomed to circle the heavens forever, often riding upside down.

Cassiopeia is an easy constellation to find. First, look for the Big Dipper. Then draw an imaginary line from the pointer stars in the Big Dipper to the North Star in the Little Bear. Now extend the line further until you reach five stars that look like a flattened "M" or "W." These stars outline the queen on her throne.

Spring Constellation

Leo: The Lion

Leo was a fierce, man-eating lion. Many hunters tried to kill Leo, but they all failed. Then the hero Hercules was asked to kill Leo. Hercules and Leo fought for thirty days. Finally, Leo ran into his cave. Hercules followed Leo and strangled him with his bare hands. Later, Zeus placed Hercules and Leo among the stars.

Summer Constellation

Cygnus: The Swan

Cygnus was a young man whose best friend was Phaethon. One day, Phaethon flew too high in his father's magic chariot. Phaethon fell off into a river and drowned. Cygnus sat by the river and wept for his friend. When the gods saw how sad Cygnus was, they felt sorry for him. They changed Cygnus into a beautiful swan. Then they placed him high in the stars.

Fall Constellation

Pegasus: The Winged Horse

Pegasus was a beautiful white horse with magic wings. Pegasus had many adventures with the hero Bellerophon. When Bellerophon died, Pegasus flew up to the heavens. You can still see him there today.

The constellation Pegasus is made up of fourteen stars. In the middle is a group of four stars called the *Great Square*. These four stars represent the body of the horse. The other stars form the neck, head, and front legs of Pegasus.

Orion: The Hunter

Orion was a giant who liked to hunt. One day he bragged that he could kill all the wild animals in the world. To teach Orion a lesson, the gods sent a scorpion to sting him. The gods then placed Orion in the sky as a constellation.

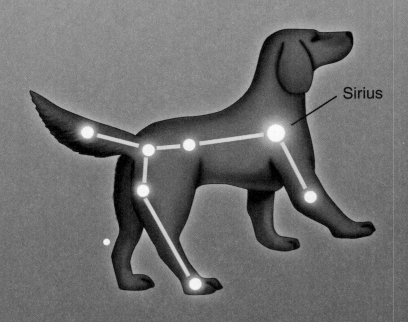

Sirius

Now look to the left of Orion in the picture.
You will see the constellation called the *Big
Dog,* or *Canis Major.* Canis Major was one
of Orion's faithful hunting dogs. *Sirius,* the
Dog Star, is part of Canis Major. This star is
the brightest of all the stars in the night sky.

Taurus: The Bull

Zeus once fell in love with a princess named Europa. The princess loved all kinds of animals. To please her, Zeus changed himself into a bull named *Taurus*. Europa was delighted with Taurus. She played with him and climbed onto his back. As soon as Europa was safely on his back, Taurus jumped into the sea and swam away with her.

That explains why the constellation Taurus is swimming. Only his head and the top part of his body can be seen above the water.

The Pleiades: Seven Sisters

Remember Orion, the giant who liked to hunt? One day, when Orion was out hunting, he saw seven beautiful sisters. The sisters were named the *Pleiades*. Orion ran after the sisters, hoping to meet them. The girls were frightened of the hunter. They called out for Zeus to help them. Zeus turned the sisters into birds so they could fly away from Orion. Later, Zeus changed the sisters into stars.

The people of Africa have other legends about the Pleiades. The Bantu people in Southern Africa believed the stars of the Pleiades looked like a plow. In East Africa, the Masai tribe thought these stars looked like a herd of cattle.

The Pleiades is a *star cluster*—a group of stars close to one another in space. The Pleiades are part of the constellation Taurus. They can be found glittering near the shoulder of the mighty bull.

If You Want to Go Stargazing

Suppose you want to look for constellations. How do you get started? First, find out which constellations will be in the sky that season and study their shapes.

Choose a clear, moonless night. If you can, find a place to stargaze far from the lights of towns or cities.

When you first go outside, wait several minutes to let your eyes adjust to the dark. Once they've adjusted, don't look directly at a streetlight or any other bright light. You may want to take along a star map and a flashlight. If you take a flashlight, cover its head with red cellophane. The red light will not change your eyes' adjustment to the dark.

Now you're all set. Good luck, and happy stargazing!